KIDS CAN DRAW & PAINT TOO!

INTRODUCTION

KIDS CAN DRAW AND PAINT TOO! is perfect for the creative child. It can unlock doors in the imagination of children and provide a medium through which they can express themselves. The instructions are easy to follow, and for those unable to read, the text can be followed visually with little or no parental guidance.

Pattern sheets or coloring book pages can be used to draw and paint. Once children develop skills and confidence in any given medium, they should be encouraged to choose their own subject matter and experiment with technique. Youngsters will be able to amuse themselves for hour upon hour; the variety of media will keep them from getting bored, although they should be encouraged to work on a project until it is completed. For the very young artist, the projects should be kept simple to eliminate potential frustration and discouragement.

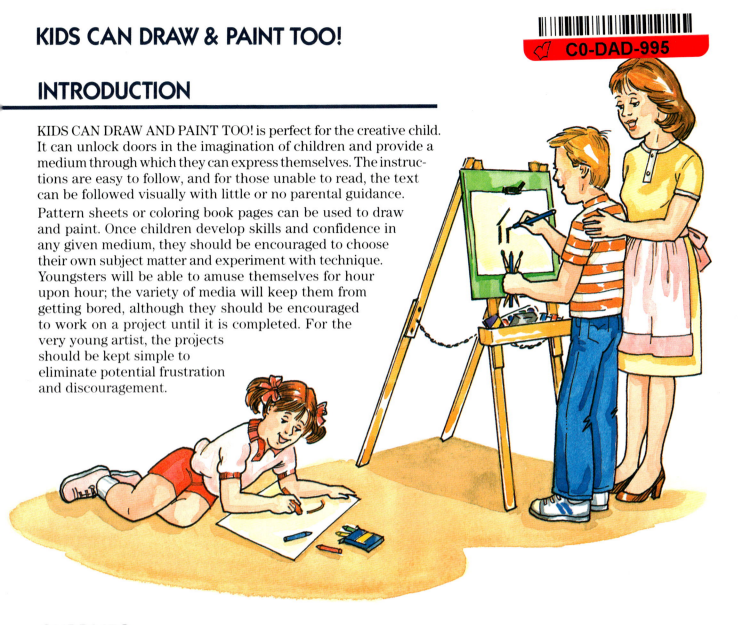

SUPPLIES

In order for your creative "Rembrandts" to try their hand at the techniques shown in this book, the following supplies will be needed: Individual sheets or a pad of multi-purpose sketching/painting paper, acrylic colors, colored chalks, oil pastels, cake watercolors, several paint brushes, several sketch pencils, rub-on letter sheet, blending stump, coloring crayons, kneaded eraser, pencil sharpener, chalkboard eraser, and a painting or drawing surface—a chalkboard easel would be ideal.

Additional items that will be needed which can be found around the home are: a cup or jar of water (for chalk drawing, acrylic painting, watercolor painting), paper towels and a bar of soap for spills and clean-up, and toothpicks.

NOTE: This book may be purchased as part of a set or independent of the set. When purchased with the set, required supplies are included. When purchased separately, supplies should be available at your local art and craft store.

NOTE TO PARENTS

Before setting your artist free, be sure to instruct him as to where to work. Choose an environment that is not "sterile" as even the most experienced artist tends to be a little messy while his imagination takes him to far away places. If necessary, cover the floors and table tops with newspaper so that if there is an accident, it will be uneventful.

Most of the media can be cleaned with soap and cold water while it is still wet; when dry even watercolor may be difficult to remove from a surface. This creative experience should be a positive one for you and your child.

DRAWING AND SKETCHING

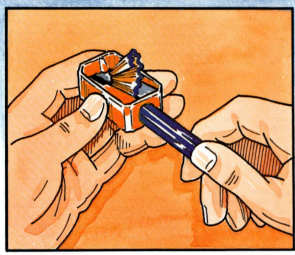

1. Sharpen a sketch pencil to a sharp point with the pencil sharpener.

2. Draw a picture of one of your favorite objects with the pencil. Do not include a lot of detail at this time.

5. Use the kneaded eraser to blend some of the tones in the shaded areas; you can add softer tones by rubbing off the lead that is on the eraser.

6. Go back and finish the detail work.

3. You can shade areas using the side of the pencil point.

4. Continue sketching using both the point for lines and the side for shading.

7. Using rub-on letters from a transfer sheet, sign your name by rubbing over the appropriate letters with the pencil.

8. You can make a card by drawing a picture on the front and then using the rub-on letter sheet for the words on the inside.

WATERCOLOR PAINTING

1. Keep the used brushes in a cup or jar of water. Always wet the brushes before you put them in paint.

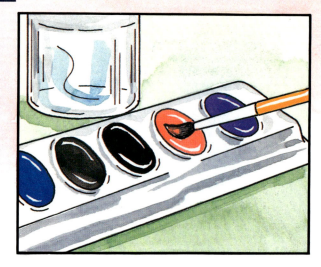

2. Apply the paint to a wet brush.

5. Try the picture on the pattern sheet and fill in the different areas with paint.

6. For the background, apply a light wash tone (remember the water).

3. Apply a wash tone with a very wet brush.

4. Blend the paint out with water.

7. Highlight certain areas with second colors or a blend of colors.

8. Sign your name using the tip of the brush.

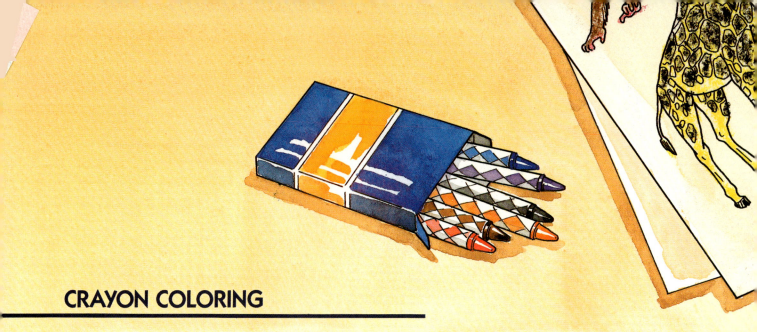

CRAYON COLORING

1. For most pictures, you can just color the objects with a crayon.

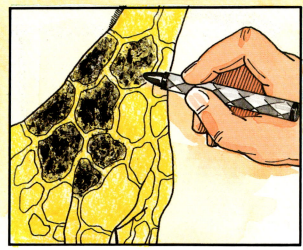

2. For a special effect, you can put colors on top of one another. Try coloring an area with a light color first and then covering it with a darker color.

5. For another interesting effect, color over an area heavily and scratch in the textured areas.

6. Apply the bottom color and then cover it with a second color. Use the blending stump to blend the colors together.

ITEM #935

ITEM #93543

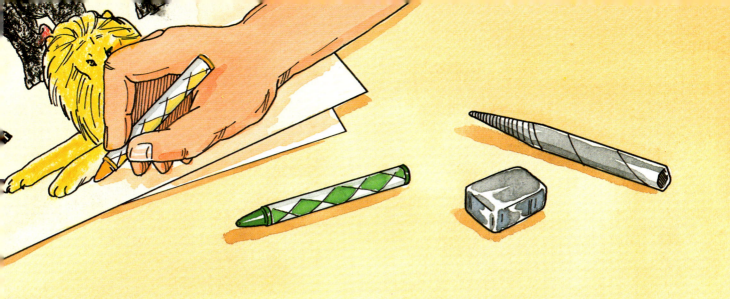

3. To add texture to an area, apply the color heavily and then scratch the textured shapes with a toothpick.

4. You can also add texture with two colors, allowing the bottom color to show through.

7. Draw your own background and then color the design.

8. Using the same animals you could try other settings—jungles, parks, zoos, or maybe a circus.

ACRYLIC PAINTING

1. Keep the used brushes in a cup or jar of water. Always wet the brushes before you put them in paint.

2. Draw the outline of your picture with one color.

5. When you don't want the colors to blend, let the first color dry thoroughly.

6. The second color will be much brighter when applied after the first layer is dry.

3. Using one color at a time, begin filling in the areas to be painted.

4. Practice blending colors using a wet brush on an already wet painting.

7. The background can be "washed out" by first applying the color and then going over it with a brush wet with water; the more water you add, the lighter the background will become.

8. Always wash your brushes with soap and water when you are through painting.

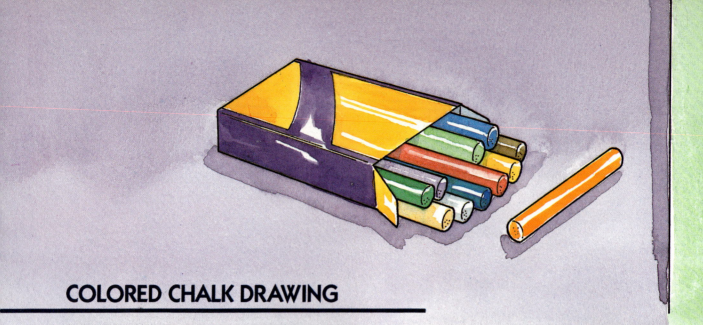

COLORED CHALK DRAWING

1. Using the chalk, draw a simple figure on the chalkboard.

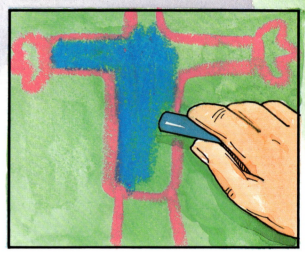

2. Fill in the areas with chalk.

5. For a textured chalk drawing, first dip the chalk in water.

6. Apply the chalk to paper using random strokes: this is not like sketching a drawing.

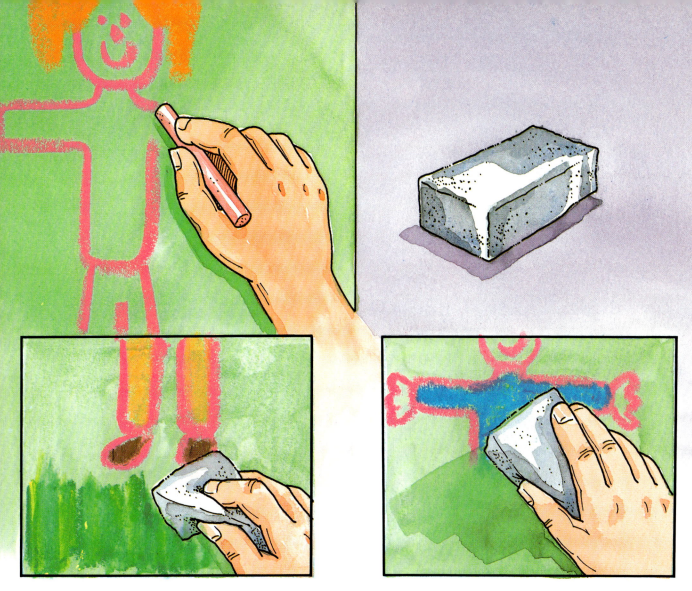

3. Use a sponge to shade areas.

4. When finished, erase the chalkboard with the chalkboard eraser.

7. After you have added a few colors, use your fingers to blend the colors.

8. Your picture will have a lovely textured effect.

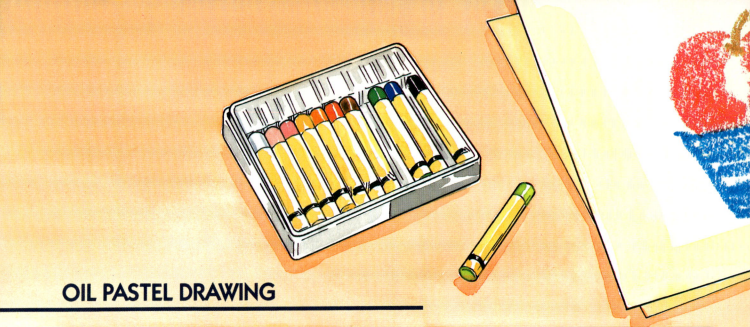

OIL PASTEL DRAWING

1. Fill in solid areas, each with a different color.

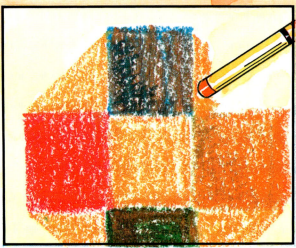

2. Go over each section with another color and observe the interesting results.

5. Try applying the pastels more lightly and use the kneaded eraser to soften certain areas.

6. You can use your fingers, rubbing lightly, to create shaded areas.